AVRO AIRCRAFT

R . T .   J A C K S O N

D0233595

ALAN SUTTON PUBLISHING LIMITED

Alan Sutton Publishing Limited
Phoenix Mill · Far Thrupp · Stroud
Gloucestershire · GL5 2BU

First published 1995

*Cover photographs: (front) the Avro Vulcan
B.Mk.2; (back) a Roe II Triplane*

British Library Cataloguing in Publication Data.
A catalogue record for this book is available from
the British Library.

ISBN 0-7509-1077-1

Typeset in 9/10 Sabon.
Typesetting and origination by
Alan Sutton Publishing Limited.
Printed in Great Britain by
Hartnolls, Bodmin, Cornwall.

To my father, the late A.J. Jackson, whose lifetime of
collecting made this book possible.

Contents

A 1913 Avro advertisement.

Introduction

A.V. Roe and Company, one of the great British aircraft manufacturing firms, was founded in 1910 by the famous aviation pioneer Alliott Verdon Roe. Over the next fifty-three years the company produced a multitude of machines, including such immortal types as the 504 trainer and the Lancaster bomber.

A.V. Roe was born at Patricroft near Manchester on 26 April 1877. At the age of fourteen he left school to take up an offer to be trained as a surveyor in British Columbia, but a recession in Canada soon forced his return to Britain. By now interested in engineering, 'A.V.' commenced a five year apprenticeship at the Lancashire and Yorkshire Railway works at Horwich in the summer of 1893. Following this he worked for a time on torpedoes at Portsmouth Dockyard before joining the merchant marine. It was while serving as third engineer on board the SS *Inchonga* on its voyages to South Africa in 1902 that Alliott first became interested in the problems of flight after observing a soaring albatross. The next few years were spent experimenting with flying models of varied designs and layout.

After leaving the sea, 'A.V.' joined the Sheffield Simplex Motor Company. Increasing success with flying models culminated in the winning of a £75 prize in a *Daily Mail* competition in April 1907. Thoughts then turned to the building of a full size aeroplane, and construction of the Roe Biplane commenced at premises in Putney owned by a brother, Dr Spencer Verdon Roe, during 1907. Trials commenced at Brooklands in mid-December 1907 with the first flight, a hop of 2 to 3 ft, being achieved on 8 June 1908.

With the construction of a triplane in mind, A.V. Roe teamed up with the engine designer J.A. Prestwich to form the JAP Avroplane Company in September 1908, but A.V. Roe's first business partnership was short lived and it was dissolved in early 1909. The larger of the two triplanes then being assembled in new premises at the railway arches at Lea Valley, Essex, was sold at auction. The remaining machine, the Roe I Triplane, was flown from the adjacent Walthamstow Marshes but, after being evicted from the railway arches later in the year, Roe moved briefly to the Old Deer Park at Richmond before moving on to Wembley Park, Middlesex, in November 1909.

Further finance was obtained from Roe's father and another brother, H.V. Roe, who was a successful businessman and proprietor of H.W. Everard and Company, the manufacturers of Bulls-Eye Braces. H.V. Roe had first become involved in Alliott's enterprise when the pair entered into partnership in April 1909, a deal which laid the foundations for the formation of A.V. Roe and Company on New Year's Day 1910.

The fledgling company's first workshops were established at the Brownsfield Mills, Ancoats, Manchester, factory of Everard & Co. The first machine to be completed was the Roe II Triplane, which took pride of place at the Manchester Aero Club's model aircraft exhibition at the White City, Manchester, on 4 March 1910. Flight testing had now been transferred to the new aerodrome in the centre of Brooklands racing track. Here the Avro Flying School was established towards the end of the year, but in October 1912 it was transferred to the quieter site of Shoreham, a move which also allowed seaplane flying from the nearby River Adur.

Back in Manchester, the company had by now recruited some talented young staff who would play a major role in the firm's success. These included R.J. Parrott, A.V. Roe's assistant and draughtsman who later became Works Manager, the skilful test pilot F.P. Raynham, and Roy Chadwick, who by the end of the First World War had become Chief Designer, a post he would hold until tragically killed in the crash of the Tudor 2 prototype at Woodford on 23 August 1947. Finance was a continual problem; early attempts to find an additional partner failed owing to aeronautics being considered a high risk investment in the days before the First World War. By the end of 1912, however, the firm was more firmly established, and backing was obtained from James Grimble Groves, a member of a leading brewing family, enabling the firm to become a limited company with £30,000 capital on 11 January 1913. Groves became Chairman with A.V. and H.V. Roe joint Managing Directors. In April 1913 the company's workshops were moved to Clifton Street, Miles Platting, Manchester. The coming of the First World War, and with it large production orders for the legendary Avro 504, resulted in a need for even larger premises. These were rented from the firm of Mather and Platt at nearby Newton Heath in September 1914 and were known as the Park Works. Meanwhile the Clifton Street works was downgraded to become the firm's woodworking department, and several sub-contractors also began producing 504s. In 1915 additional Avro works were established at Heath Street, Newton Heath (burned down in May 1918) and the Empire Works, Failsworth. By the war's end over 8,000 504s had been produced.

In 1916 the decision was made to establish a factory at Hamble, near Southampton, the waterside location being deliberately chosen to allow the development of seaplanes. At Hamble it was intended to build not only the works hangar but also a garden city for the workers. This latter scheme, though, had to be abandoned after only a few houses had been completed because of the wartime shortage of building materials. With R.J. Parrott as General Manager the Hamble Works took on the role of experimental shop after production orders were not forthcoming for either the Avro 529 bomber or type 530 fighter. This setback thwarted a scheme to start a separate company, A.V. Roe (Southampton) Ltd.

The armistice in November 1918 resulted in the wholesale cancellation of contracts and the company fortunes took a major turn for the worse. Many workers were laid off and the firm was forced to diversify into the making of such items as prams and billiard tables. Plans were also set to move into the motor business and a small 10 hp car was designed. However, in May 1920

Crossley Motors took a controlling interest in A.V. Roe and Co. Ltd and production of the car was halted after only a few examples had been completed. It was intended that Crossley car bodies would be made instead, but the recession in the motor industry meant that this scheme did not go ahead.

In a further effort to increase post-war revenue the company set up a joyriding operation, The Avro Transport Company, in 1919 to take advantage of the keen public interest in flying. The company, which used Avro 536s and war surplus Avro 504Ks, was based at Alexandra Park aerodrome, Manchester, but joyriding sites were also established at a number of coastal resorts. The company also had the distinction of operating Britain's first scheduled domestic air service, which began on 24 May 1919. The success of joyriding in 1919 was soon history, however, and by April 1920 the deepening economic recession meant that customers were few and the enterprise was wound up.

In August 1920 A.V. Roe and Co. Ltd moved its headquarters to Newton Heath, Manchester. Test flying continued at Alexandra Park until the Air Ministry's lease on the airfield expired in 1924. Land was then acquired at New Hall Farm and this became Woodford Aerodrome, which remains in use by British Aerospace today.

Small production orders for Avro 504Ks and the refurbishment of others for the RAF and overseas air forces kept the company alive during the difficult years of the early twenties.

A.V. Roe himself left the company in 1928 after selling his shares to Sir John Siddeley, later Lord Kenilworth, head of the Armstrong Siddeley Development Company. 'A.V.' was knighted in 1929, becoming Sir Alliott Verdon-Roe, and took control of the Isle of Wight boatbuilders S.E. Saunders Ltd. Renamed Saunders-Roe Ltd the company was soon engaged in the production of flying boats. Sir Alliott was still president of the firm when he died on 4 January 1958.

The takeover by the Armstrong Siddeley group resulted in the Avro design office moving from Hamble to Manchester and the works were sold to Air Service Training in April 1931. The last years at Hamble were noteworthy for experiments with Cierva designed autogiros, several of which were given Avro designations. Later, in early 1934, a licence was obtained to build the Cierva C.30A, and seventy-seven examples were built at Newton Heath. Links with another foreign company, the Dutch firm Fokker, were established in 1928, and these resulted in the building of the eight passenger Avro 618 Ten, a modified version of the Fokker F.VIIb/3m, the scaled down four passenger Avro 619 Five, the Avro 624 Six and the high wing Avro 642 Eighteen. With orders being received from home and overseas for Avians, Tutors, 626s and Cadets, the company returned to prosperity in the early 1930s.

In July 1935 A.V. Roe and Co. Ltd became a subsidiary of the newly created Hawker Siddeley Aircraft Company. Expansion of the RAF in the mid-thirties, prompted by political tension in Europe, resulted in orders being received for 174 Hawker Audax biplanes as well as Avro designed machines, which by now included the famous Avro 652A Anson. The expansion in aircraft production also resulted in the establishment of government sponsored aircraft factories. One of these, at Chadderton, near Manchester, was handed over to the Avro company in 1938 and was first used to fulfil an order for

Bristol Blenheim IV light bombers, 1,005 of which were eventually built by Avro, with production finishing in November 1941.

By the outbreak of war in September 1939 twin-engined Manchester heavy bombers were in full production, as well as Blenheims and Ansons. All final assembly was transferred to new hangars erected at the firm's Woodford aerodrome where new production facilities were also built. Use was also made of hangar space at Manchester's Ringway Airport, most notably for the assembly of the prototype Lancaster which made its first flight there on 9 January 1941. Mass production of the Lancaster was soon under way and a total of 7,374 were ultimately built by Avro and a number of sub-contractors, including Victory Aircraft in Canada. Additional production facilities were opened at Yeadon Airport, Leeds. Here production of Ansons continued throughout the war, reaching 130 aircraft a month during 1943 and 1944. By the time the last of the type rolled off the assembly lines in May 1952 some 11,020 had been built, including 2,881 in Canada. The York transport aircraft was another wartime design, being first flown on 5 July 1942, but the shortage of materials and the priority given to bomber production meant that relatively few aircraft were produced until hostilities ended. One specially equipped York was used as a flying conference room by the Prime Minister, Winston Churchill.

After the Second World War, the company again contracted and civil types such as Yorks, Tudors and Lancastrians rolled off the production lines, as well as military machines including by then the Lincoln bomber.

Victory Aircraft in Canada, which had produced Ansons and Lancasters in addition to single examples of the York and Lincoln, was taken over late in 1945 and renamed A.V. Roe Canada Ltd. However, only one of its designs, the Avro Canada CF-100 Canuck, went into series production.

Back in Manchester, the Shackleton maritime aircraft, a type which was destined to remain in RAF service for over forty years, first appeared in 1949 and the impressive delta wing Vulcan, the company's first jet design, in 1952. This famous aircraft formed (together with the Handley-Page Victor and Vickers Valiant) Britain's V-bomber force, and the B.Mk.2 version was equipped with the Avro Blue Steel stand-off nuclear bomb from 1962. Avro aircraft also built seventy-five English Electric Canberras.

By the end of the 1950s the company only retained the Woodford and Chadderton factories. It was in 1963 that the end came for the Avro name when on 1 July, following a re-organisation, the company became the Avro-Whitworth division of Hawker Siddeley Aviation Ltd. The Avro 748 airliner then in production was redesignated the Hawker Siddeley HS.748.

Some thirty years after the great name of Avro had been dropped it reappeared when Hawker Siddeley's successor British Aerospace formed a new subsidiary, Avro International Aerospace, to produce regional jets. These were updated versions of the British Aerospace 146, production of which had been transferred from Hatfield to Woodford.

R.T. Jackson
Leigh-on-Sea
June 1995

THE PIONEER
YEARS (1908–14)

A.V. Roe with the model that won the highest awarded prize of £75 in the Daily Mail-
sponsored model aeroplane competition of April 1907. Roe had been inspired by the sight
of a soaring albatross to begin experimenting with flying models in 1902.

After being built at Putney, A.V. Roe's first full size aeroplane, the Roe I biplane, was taken to Brooklands in September 1907 where it was housed in the 'Avroplane' shed. Roe planned to try for the £2,500 prize offered for the first flight round the 3 mile Brooklands circuit, and the £1,000 offered for a mile long flight with a passenger aboard.

The Roe I biplane's 6 hp JAP engine gave insufficient power and it flew only when towed by a car. Straight flights were successful but turns resulted in mishaps, until a quick release was designed which allowed controlled landings. Lift, it was thought, was only generated by pressure on the undersurfaces so there was no top wing covering.

In May 1908, the loan of a 24 hp Antoinette engine was arranged, and after alterations to the wings and propeller Roe succeeded in taking the biplane off under its own power on 8 June 1908. Hops were made to a height of 2 to 3 ft, but Roe did not publicise the event and his claim to be the first to fly in Britain was disallowed in 1928.

Construction of the Roe I Triplane began in early 1909. Fitted with a 10 hp JAP, the machine made its first hops at Walthamstow Marshes on 5 June 1909. It was labelled the Bullseye Avroplane on account of its sponsorship by H.V. Roe's braces company.

A.V. Roe in the Bullseye Avroplane at the Blackpool Flying Meeting of October 1909. There the Triplane reached a height of 150 ft. The craft is now in the Science Museum.

The second Roe I Triplane flying at Wembley in December 1909. The 20 hp JAP engine improved the performance enough to allow circuits of the airfield with few mishaps.

The second Roe I Triplane in modified form at Brooklands, where it was flown in this guise in the flying competition on Easter Monday, 28 March 1910. Dubbed 'The Two-and-a-Bit Plane', it had several design features from the Roe II incorporated, but it quickly became outmoded and was withdrawn from use after only a few weeks.

The Roe II triplane at the Olympia Aero Show in March 1910. The Roe II was fitted with a 35 hp Green water-cooled engine and was named Mercury by the daughter of the Lord Mayor while displayed at the Manchester Aero Club exhibition earlier the same month. Flight trials took place at Brooklands but it twice rolled on take off and landed inverted.

Mercury was fitted with ailerons in place of the original wing warping during April 1910. This, however, did not entirely halt the mishaps such as this one which occurred towards the end of 1910. A second Roe II biplane was made for W.G. Windham, later Sir Walter Windham MP, and delivered to Brooklands in May 1910.

Four Roe III Triplanes were built, the prototype powered by a 35 hp JAP and the other three by 35 hp Greens. One Roe III was sold to Harvard University Aeronautical Society and flown by Roe at the Harvard Flying Meeting at Boston in September 1911, after his own Green powered machine, which had been specially shipped to the USA, crashed.

Roe flying the third Roe III triplane at the Blackpool Flying Meeting in August 1910. This machine was built in only a few days after the second Roe III, which had been used by the Avro Flying School, was destroyed by fire together with the Roe II Mercury while they were en route by rail from Weybridge to Blackpool.

The 35 hp Green powered Roe IV Triplane was completed in September 1910 and used by the Avro Flying School at Brooklands. It was considered more difficult to fly than earlier machines and was involved in many mishaps. Several famous pilots, including the then Avro mechanic C. Howard Pixton, obtained their flying certificates on the Roe IV.

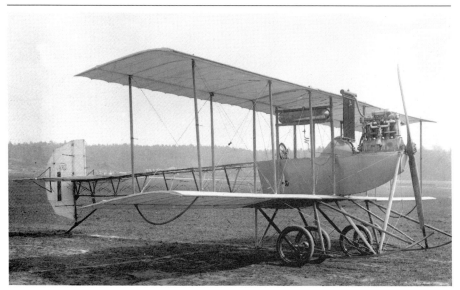

The prototype Avro Type D biplane was first flown by C. Howard Pixton at Brooklands on 1 April 1911. The same pilot flew the 35 hp Green engined machine, which was considered easy to fly, in the Brooklands to Shoreham Air Race of 6 May 1911.

A special 60 hp ENV engined sesquiplane Type D was built to compete in the £10,000 *Daily Mail* Circuit of Britain Race. It was constructed at Manchester and first flown by R.C. Kemp at Brooklands on 18 July 1911. The machine was destroyed four days later on the morning of the race, when part of the port lower mainplane failed at 150 ft.

The Avro Flying School, which used the third Type D, moved from Brooklands to Shoreham in October 1912. Among the group with the machine at Shoreham are A.E. Geere, the Chief Flying Instructor (extreme left), and Cecil Pashley (standing in front of the pilot), who was still flying as CFI of the Southern Aero Club as late as 1965.

Avro's test pilot F.P. Raynham in the fourth Type D, a single seater with a specially tuned 45 hp Green engine, at Brooklands in October 1911. Raynham hoped to win the Michelin speed and long distance prizes but was unsuccessful in both, the machine finally coming to grief on 27 October, when it forced landed in Brookland's sewage farm.

The fifth Type D, an improved sesquiplane version with a 35 hp Green engine. There were two further Type Ds, No. 6 with a 35 hp Vialle and No. 7 with a 50 hp Isaacson. The former was first flown at Brooklands by F.P. Raynham on 20 November 1911, while the latter was completed in the Brownsfield Mills works, by 29 November 1911.

The original Type D was acquired by Cdr. Schwann (later AVM Sir Oliver Schwann KCB, CBE) for £700 in June 1911. It was taken by rail to Barrow-in-Furness where a number of Schwann-designed float undercarriages were tried. After several mishaps, on 9 April 1912 it became the first British seaplane to take off from British waters.

Capt. E.W. Wakefield of Kendal ordered a Curtiss biplane from A.V. Roe and Co., which was delivered to Brooklands in May 1911. In July it was delivered to its owner at Lake Windermere. Here the wheels were replaced by a float undercarriage, and H. Stanley Adams tested the machine, later known as the Lakes Water Bird, that November.

The Avro Farman-type under construction in 1911. The machine was built for Maurice F. Edwards, a Bolton businessman, who was responsible for manufacturing Avro aero engines. Only a few Avro 20 hp two-cylinder air-cooled engines were built, and it was one of these that powered the Farman.

John R. Duigan, an Australian, placed an order for a private aeroplane in the summer of 1911. The Duigan biplane was initially fitted with a 40 hp Alveston, but after attempts by Duigan to fly at Huntingdon were unsuccessful this was replaced by a 35 hp ENV. Though underpowered, the machine subsequently flew successfully at Brooklands.

After John Duigan had successfully obtained his Aviator's Certificate and completed several hours flying in his biplane, he returned home and the machine was sold to the Lakes Flying Company. It was delivered to Windermere in June 1912 where it was rebuilt as the 50 hp Gnome powered Lakes Seabird. The machine was used for joyriding.

The Burga monoplane was designed by Lt. Burga of the Peruvian Navy and incorporated some of his novel flying controls. Lateral control was achieved not by wing warping but by use of two rudders, one above and one below the fuselage which worked in opposite directions. The Burga was built at Brownsfield Mills and delivered to Shoreham where it was first flown by H.R. Simms on 20 November 1912. It was considered fast and climbed well, but was badly damaged when it crashed in December 1912.

The Avro Type E prototype under construction at Brownsfield Mills early in 1912, with the Burga monoplane visible in the background. The Type E was built to meet the first War Office specification for a two-seater aircraft with a maximum speed of 55 mph, an initial climb of 200 ft/min, able to maintain 4,500 ft for one hour and carry a 350 lb load.

The Type E prototype, which was powered by a 60 hp ENV water-cooled engine, was first flown by Wilfred Parke at Brooklands on 3 March 1912. For a time it was used as a testbed for a new 60 hp ABC engine, but with the ENV re-installed it was sent to the Avro School at Shoreham, where it was destroyed in a fatal crash on 29 June 1913.

J. Laurence Hall with his Avro 500, which was delivered to Hendon on 22 January 1914 and used for displays and instruction. The Avro 500 was essentially a 50 hp Gnome powered Type E, the comma rudder only appearing on later models. The Portuguese Government acquired one Type E while another was kept as a demonstrator.

The Type 500 was regarded by A.V. Roe as his first really successful aeroplane and the War Office were also impressed, buying the prototype and ordering two others with dual control. These went to the Central Flying School at Upavon as did four others, including 448, which were ordered in December 1912. The Admiralty acquired two others.

The Avro 502 single seater was known as the Type Es to distinguish it from the two-seat Type E (Avro 500). Five Avro 502s were ordered and were all delivered to No. 3 Squadron at Netheravon by June 1913. They had all been transferred to No. 5 Squadron at Farnborough by January 1914 and were all in use at Upavon by September 1914.

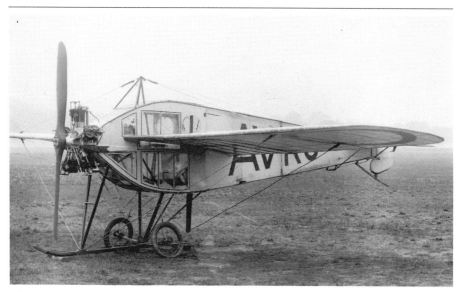

The single-seat Avro Type F was powered by a 35 hp Vialle. It was first flown by Wilfred Parke at Brooklands on 1 May 1912 and was the first enclosed cockpit aircraft ever to fly. The aircraft forced landed at Weybridge on 25 May owing to engine failure and did not fly again until September, when it turned over on landing and was badly damaged.

The two-seat Type G was built for the August 1912 Military Aircraft Competition at Larkhill. Two Type Gs, No. 6 and No. 7, were built but only the latter, fitted with a 60 hp Green, competed in the trials. Of note is that while flying the Type G Wilfred Parke was successful in pulling out of a spin, or Parke's Dive as it was subsequently known.

The Avro 501 was originally built as an amphibian with a central float with tricycle undercarriage. This unit was replaced with twin floats without wheels, and in this guise it was delivered to the Admiralty's Isle of Grain experimental station and given the naval serial 16. The floats proved too heavy and the 100 hp Gnome powered machine was reconfigured as a landplane. Flown by F.P. Raynham, it passed its acceptance tests at RNAS Eastchurch on 28 August 1913 and served there as a trainer until early 1916.

The prototype Avro 503, or Type H as it was originally called, at Shoreham in June 1913. Powered by a 100 hp Gnome the machine performed well, and after test flying it was sold to the German Government and given the serial D12. On 13 September the machine became the first aircraft to fly the 40 miles from Wilhelmshaven to Heligoland.

Avro 503 landplane 52 at RNAS Chingford in 1915. The Admiralty ordered three 503s for use by the Royal Naval Air Service and these were delivered to the Isle of Grain in late 1913. After a year all three were converted to landplanes and served as trainers.

The prototype Avro 504 at Hendon in September 1913, in its original form with warping ailerons. Flown for the first time on 18 September 1913, the 80 hp Gnome powered machine was very advanced for its time and averaged an impressive 66.5 mph when flown by F.P. Raynham into fourth place in the Aerial Derby at Hendon three days later.

F.P. Raynham with his passenger H.V. Roe, left, before the start of the race between the 504 and the Blackburn Type I, flown by Robert Blackburn, on 2 October 1913. Resulting from a challenge made by Blackburn after the Aerial Derby, the race was to have been over a 100 mile course starting and finishing at Leeds.

F.P. Raynham (right), Avro's talented test pilot, joined the firm in 1911 after learning to fly with the Avro Flying School at Brooklands. The race with the Blackburn was cut short when the Avro 504 was forced down near Barnsley by poor visibility. Later it was modified at Manchester to take streamlined cowlings and fitted with ailerons.

The 504 prototype at the Clifton Street works in seaplane form in early 1914. After being flown as a landplane from Brooklands, the 504 was sold to the *Daily Mail* and a twin float undercarriage built which could be interchanged with wheels as required. As a seaplane the machine was used for joyriding at coastal resorts until the outbreak of war.

Production of the Avro 504 began in the summer of 1913 after the War Office ordered twelve. Before the outbreak of war on 4 August 1914, at least four others, for civil customers or for demonstration use, were built as well as one machine, 179, for the Admiralty. One of the civil customers was Harold Blackburn.

The Avro 508 at the Olympia Aero Show in March 1914. The 80 hp Gnome powered reconnaissance pusher aircraft was completed in December 1913 and delivered to Brooklands the following month. No orders were forthcoming but the machine was still operational at Brooklands in April 1915.

The Avro 510 prototype at Calshott in July 1914. The 150 hp Sunbeam Nubian powered seaplane was built for the Circuit of Britain Race, which was cancelled owing to the outbreak of war. After some test flying, which showed the design of the float to be particularly good, it was bought by the Admiralty, who also ordered a further five.

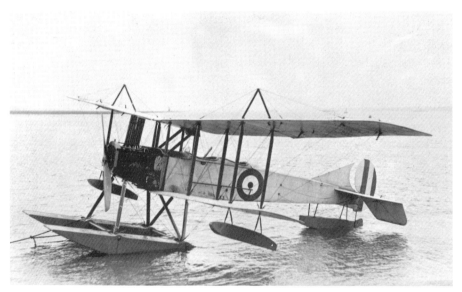

The production Avro 510s were delivered to RNAS between December 1914 and April 1915, three to Killingholme and two to Dundee. Their performance was very poor, however, and they failed the acceptance tests. Four were sent to the Supermarine works at Woolston for modifications in October 1915 and all were grounded by March 1916.

The Avro 511 was due to have been flown in the Aerial Derby race round London on 23 May 1914, but this was postponed until 6 June because of bad weather. The machine was reconfigured as the Avro 514 with straight wings for the rescheduled race, but was badly damaged at Brooklands while taxiing out to fly to the starting point, Hendon.

Avro 511, which was intended to be a single-seat military scout, in company with a production Avro 504 seaplane on the Avro stand at the Olympia Aero Show in March 1914. Following its mishap at Brooklands, the machine was repaired at Manchester and subsequently flown at Southport Sands, the war preventing any further development.

THE FIRST WORLD WAR (1914–18)

Flt. Lt. S.V. Sippe, with his aircraft, the Avro 504 873, which was used together with 874 and 875 to launch a bombing raid against the Zeppelin sheds at Freidrichshafen on 21 November 1914. A fourth machine, 179, suffered damage and did not join the raid.

873 at Belfort, France, before departing on the Freidrichshafen raid, the most famous of the few offensive actions involving the Avro 504. Equipped with four 20 lb bombs the three 504s caused some damage to the Zeppelin sheds and destroyed the gas plant.

During the Freidrichshafen raid 874, piloted by Sqdn. Cdr. E. Featherstone Briggs, was shot down and the aircraft taken to the German workshops at Adlershof where its tail can be seen on the right. Sippe and Flt. Cdr. J.T. Babington in 875 were able to return to Belfort, 125 miles away, where they landed safely after being airborne for four hours.

The main role of the 504 and its variants during the type's long service career was as a trainer. The dual-control Avro 504A was a strengthened version of the basic 504 with reduced span ailerons which was built in considerable numbers for the RFC. As with other major variants, batches were built by sub-contractors as well as A.V. Roe.

The Avro 504B was a much modified version with large rudder and dorsal fin for the RNAS. A few 504Bs were used operationally with forward firing guns while late production machines were provided with a scarff ring gun mount in the rear cockpit and 80 hp Le Rhône engine in place of the usual 80 hp Gnome.

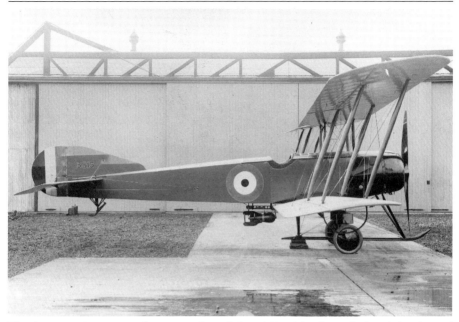

The Avro 504C was a single-seat version of the 504B with a large fuel tank in place of the front cockpit which gave 8 hours' endurance. It was used for coastal reconnaissance and in an anti-Zeppelin role, for which it was fitted with a Lewis gun which could fire incendiary ammunition at 45 degrees upwards. Bombs could also be carried.

The Avro 504D, only six of which were built, was the RFC version of the 504C but with a comma style rudder. The first 504D was delivered in August 1915.

A development of the 504B, the Avro 504E was fitted with the more powerful 100 hp Gnome Monosoupape engine, the rear cockpit moved aft and an extra fuel tank fitted ahead of it behind the front cockpit. Only ten 504Es were delivered to the RNAS and the type saw service at Chingford, Cranwell and Fairlop.

The unique Avro 504F 8603 was an Avro 504C fitted with a 75 hp Rolls-Royce Hawk six-cylinder engine. A production order for thirty Avro 504Fs was cancelled. The Avro 504G was a modified version of the 504B equipped with guns and bomb racks for training while the single 504H was a strengthened 504C used for catapult launch trials.

The Avro 504J was a 504A fitted with the more powerful 100 hp Gnome Monosoupape engine. Production began in 1916 and many aircraft ordered as 504As were completed as 504Js. The variant became the standard RFC training aircraft.

Avro 504J fuselages awaiting delivery outside the Avro factory at Newton Heath, Manchester, premises which were rented from the firm of Mather and Platt. The 504J, which was fully aerobatic, was mass produced to meet the RFC's training requirement.

The School of Special Flying at Gosport was one of the first units to receive Avro 504Js. It was founded in July 1917 by Maj. R.R. Smith-Barry, who developed a new training method which involved use of the 'Gosport' inter-cockpit speaking tube.

One Avro 504J flew with single-bay reduced span wings at Gosport in January 1918.

Towards the end of 1917, with production of the Gnome Monosoupape being run down, there was a need to fit alternative powerplants. The front end of the 504J was therefore modified to accept 110 hp Le Rhônes and 130 hp Le Clergets, and in this form became the famous Avro 504K. Several thousand were built.

In early 1918 Avro 504K single-seat fighter conversions were introduced to replace FE.2bs in some northern home defence squadrons. These 110 hp Le Rhône powered machines were fitted with Lewis guns mounted above the centre section and had an impressive ceiling of 18,000 ft. Five squadrons still had 504K fighters at the war's end.

An Avro 504K with a Hucks starter. With the advent of higher power engines, starting by hand swinging became more difficult so the pioneer aviator B.C. Hucks designed a motorised starter, which was mounted on a Ford Model T car chassis. It engaged with a starter dog on the propeller hub and automatically disengaged when the engine started.

In 1918 500 Clerget engined Avro 504Ks were ordered from Canadian Aeroplanes Ltd of Toronto, but only two had been completed before the war, and therefore production ended. The Canadian Avro 504K had the V-type undercarriage that was fitted to some British home defence fighter versions but was unique in having a central bracing strut.

Two Avro 519 150 hp Sunbeam Nubian powered single-seat folding-wing biplane bombers were built for the RNAS in 1916. Trials showed the performance to be poor and 225 hp Sunbeam engines were later fitted. There were no production orders.

The RFC version of the Avro 519 was the two-seat 225 hp Sunbeam engined Avro 519A. Two were ordered but the type's poor performance, particularly its rate of climb, led to the second machine being completed as the type 522. The large centre section radiator would have obscured the pilot's forward view as well as producing drag.

Developed from the Avro 504, the Avro 521 was a 110 hp Clerget powered fighter-trainer armed with a rear cockpit Lewis gun. F.P. Raynham, who test flew the machine at Trafford Park, Manchester, found it to be unstable and unpleasant to fly. It was, however, delivered to Farnborough in February 1916 and afterwards went to the Central Flying School at Upavon where it crashed, killing the pilot, on 21 September 1916.

The Avro 521A had 42 ft span wings compared to those of 30 ft fitted to the standard type 521. A production order for twenty-five standard Avro 521s was cancelled after the type was found to be difficult to fly and prone to going into a spin off a right-hand turn.

Originally ordered by the RFC as a type 519A, the 225 hp Sunbeam powered Avro 522 differed from the earlier type in that it had equal span wings and the large radiator was repositioned to the side of the fuselage. The machine was sent to Hamble from Manchester on 1 November 1916 and remained there until April 1917.

The Avro 523 Pike, left, with the Avro 523A at Hamble in March 1917. The 523 was a multi-role bomber-cum-photo reconnaissance fighter powered by twin 160 hp Sunbeam pusher engines. Though performance was good production orders went to other types. The 150 hp Green powered 523A was originally built as a pusher but after tests at Southport Sands in August 1916 it was rebuilt in tractor configuration.

Powered by a 150 hp Sunbeam engine, the Avro 527 was designed in December 1915 as a reconnaissance fighter for the RFC, and was armed with a Lewis gun mounted in the rear cockpit. It was tested at Farnborough in early 1916 but performance was poor.

Developed from the type 519, the Avro 528 Silver King bomber was built at Newton Heath and sent to Hamble for trials in September 1916. Its 250 hp Sunbeam gave trouble and though a new engine and alternative propellers were tried problems continued, resulting in the Admiralty refusing to accept the machine.

The Avro 529 was a larger version of the Avro 523 Pike, powered by two 190 hp Rolls-Royce Falcons. Two machines, one of which was completed as the 529A, were ordered by the Admiralty in 1916 and were intended for use by the RNAS as long range bombers. The 529 was built at Manchester and first flown at Hamble in March 1917.

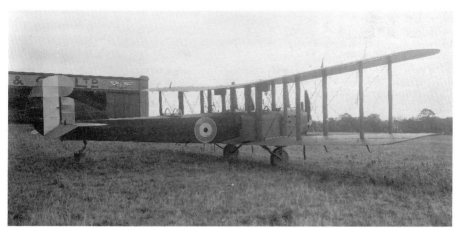

The Avro 529A was powered by two 230 hp BHP engines housed in low slung nacelles. It could carry twenty 50 lb bombs mounted vertically inside the fuselage. The aircraft went to Martlesham Heath for trials, where it crashed when the rudder gave way on 11 November 1917. Though performance was good there were no production orders.

The prototype Avro 530 fighter in its original form with small fin and rudder being assembled at Hamble. The aircraft was first flown in July 1917 powered by a 200 hp Hispano-Suiza engine rather than the 300 hp Hispano-Suiza for which it was designed, as there were none of these available. Despite the lower power performance was good.

The prototype Avro 530 outside the Hamble works in modified form, with streamlined front end, faired undercarriage and larger fin and rudder. The aircraft was flown from the front cockpit with a gunner occupying the rear seat. There were no production orders as new 200 hp Hispano-Suizas were required for SE.5As, there were no alternatives available, and the rival Bristol Fighter was already in production.

Only two Avro 530s were built. The second machine had different mainplanes from the first and was powered by a 200 hp Sunbeam Arab.

The Avro 531 Spider was a private venture lightweight fighter that made use of many Avro 504K components. It was first flown at Hamble in April 1918 powered by a 110 hp Le Rhône though a 130 hp Clerget was later fitted. The machine was flown by pilots of the School of Special Flying at Gosport in early 1918 and it performed very well, but no orders were received as the Sopwith Snipe had already been selected by the RAF. The Spider was still in use for experimental purposes at Alexandra Park in 1919.

The Avro 533 Manchester was a three-seat twin-engined bomber or photo reconnaissance fighter. Developed from the Avro 529 and built at Hamble towards the end of 1918, the Manchester I was powered by two 320 hp ABC Dragonfly engines.

Non-availability of Dragonfly engines resulted in the first Manchester being completed as a Mk.II with two 300 hp Siddeley Pumas. It first flew at Hamble in December 1918, but despite performing well the war had ended and with it the need for such a bomber. A Manchester III, complete except for its 400 hp Liberty engines, was scrapped.

BETWEEN THE WARS (1919–39) – MORE AVRO 504S

An Avro 504K of the Avro Transport Company joyriding at Southport in 1919. With the war over and the cutbacks in aircraft production, new sources of income were sought and the Avro Transport Company was formed to exploit the keen public interest in flying.

An ATC Avro 504K taking off from Alexandra Park Aerodrome, Manchester. Britain's first domestic scheduled air service, from Alexandra Park to Southport, was inaugurated on 24 May 1919. The Avro Transport Company closed and the fleet of Avro 504Ks was sold in April 1920, as the deepening depression meant that joyriding customers were few.

Two Avro 504K seaplanes outside the Avro Transport Company's base at Cockshot Point on Lake Windermere in 1919. As well as joyriding throughout the season, C. Howard Pixton, who in earlier times had been with the Avro Flying School at Brooklands, flew newspapers to the Isle of Man during August and September 1919.

Based at Croydon, The Aircraft Disposal Company overhauled a large number of war-surplus Avro 504Ks for sale to overseas military and civil owners. In addition, in 1919 and 1920 the British Government gave Imperial Gift Avro 504Ks to Australia, Canada, India, New Zealand and South Africa. A.V. Roe and Co. and Vickers were also engaged in overhauling and supplying surplus Avro 504Ks to foreign customers.

Avro 504K fuselages stacked inside the Aircraft Disposal Company's works at Croydon. The aircraft were stripped and rebuilt in a production hall, emerging in an as-new state.

G-AUBG, the first of nine 100 hp Sunbeam Dyak powered Avro 504Ks built by the Australian Aircraft and Engineering Co. Ltd. The Mascot, NSW-based company was founded by H.E. Broadsmith, the former manager of Avro's Manchester works.

One of the founders of QANTAS, P.J. McGinnis, left, and a passenger in front of Dyak Avro 504K G-AUBG, the first aircraft acquired by the company that is now the Australian national airline. The machine cost £1,500 and McGinnis flew it from Mascot to Longreach, Queensland, on 21 January 1921.

Avro 504Ks, initially powered by 150 hp Bentley BR.1s, were built in Japan after they acquired manufacturing rights for £30,000. Other 504Ks were built in Belgium and in The Dutch East Indies.

The Royal Aircraft Establishment used a number of Avro 504Ks for experimental flying, including F8940, which had modified tail surfaces for low speed lateral control tests in 1922. It also had the V-type undercarriage used on some 504K Home Defence Fighters.

The Norwegian Avro 504K N-37 was converted in 1929 to take a 140 hp Hispano-Suiza HS.8a water-cooled engine and fitted with a cabin top.

An Avro 504K with a 100 hp Green. Many different powerplants were fitted to Avro 504Ks including, for test purposes by the RAE, a 170 hp ABC Wasp I.

A number of joyriding concerns sprang up when civil flying recommenced at Easter 1919. They made use of surplus Avro 504Ks which initially carried their former military serials as registrations. The Navarro Aviation Company's Avro 504K D9304, later G-EAEA, was at Whitstable, Kent, in the summer of 1919. It was sold in May 1920.

Formed in 1920, the Berkshire Aviation Co. was the forerunner of Berkshire Aviation Tours, one of the great names of early 1920s joyriding. With their Avro 504K, G-EAKX, at Alexandra Park are (from right to left) J.C.C. Taylor, formerly an Avro apprentice and the Avro Transport Company's Chief Engineer, A.L. Robinson, who later flew for Imperial Airways, J.D.V. Holmes, involved along with his brother F.J.V. Holmes, and an unidentified individual.

Percival Philips, right, who founded The Cornwall Aviation Co. in 1924, posing with an engineer, B.P.M. Swan, in front of the joyriding company's famous Avro 504K G-EBIZ at Enfield. By 1931 the company had carried 95,000 passengers at sites throughout southern England. Of these, 55,100 had been flown by Capt. Philips himself.

Wingwalking was a feature of air shows between the wars. Martin Hearn, the legendary exponent of the art, is atop Aviation Tours' Avro 504K G-EBYW in the early 1930s.

The 100 hp Gnome Monosoupape powered Avro 504K Mk.II was produced at Hamble in 1924. It had Avro 504N undercarriage and wings and, though none were sold, the intention was to supply conversion kits to allow foreign air forces to update their existing 504Ks. Similar machines, known as Avro Anuhuacs, were built in Mexico.

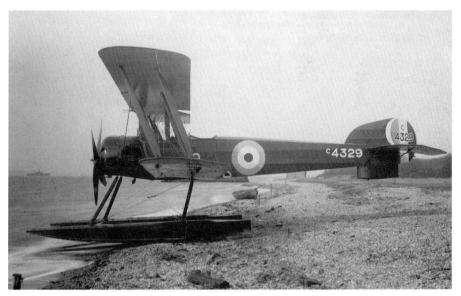

The prototype 130 hp Clerget powered Avro 504L seaplane at Hamble in 1919. Seven 150 hp Bentley BR.1 powered 504Ls were produced at Hamble for the Avro Transport Company, and 504Ks were converted by A.V. Roe at Manchester and by the Eastbourne Aviation Company. Others flew in Australia, Canada, Japan, New Zealand and Sweden.

The Eastbourne Aviation Company used six three-seat Avro 504Ls for joyriding along the south coast in 1919 and 1920. Three took part in a race at Hove in August 1920.

In 1921 the Imperial Japanese Navy received ten Hamble-built Avro 504Ls and following the acquisition of manufacturing rights others were built by the Nakajima Aircraft Manufacturing Company. All were powered by Bentley BR.1 rotary engines.

Built in April 1919, the Avro 504M was a three-seat cabin conversion of the 504K powered by a 100 hp Gnome Monosoupape. It was used by Avro for charters and joyriding and was extensively used to carry newspapers during the railway strike of autumn 1919. At least one Avro 504M copy known as the Aiba Tsubami IV was built in Japan.

The Avro 504M featured widely in the press when it was used to take a newly wed couple from the church at Chorley Wood, Bucks, to their honeymoon in Cornwall, on 26 June 1919. This exploit earned the 504M the unofficial name of Avro Limousine.

Before the advent of the definitive Avro 504N there were a number of 504K conversions incorporating features of the later mark. In 1922 E9265 and E9266 were fitted with 150 hp Armstrong Siddeley Lynx radials but retained the skid undercarriage.

J733, one of two aircraft ordered by the Air Ministry in 1924, was the first machine to incorporate all the features of the Avro 504N, which included the N-type undercarriage, twin 18 gallon fuel tanks and airframe modifications. It was powered by a 100 hp Bristol Lucifer while its sister machine, J750, had a 180 hp Armstrong Siddeley Lynx. 511 production Avro 504Ns trainers were built for the RAF between 1927 and 1932.

The Aircraft Disposal Company produced four Bristol Lucifer engined Avro 504Ns for Argentina. Around one hundred RAF Avro 504Ks were converted to 504Ns, there were also civil conversions, and A.V. Roe built new military 504Ns for Belgium, Brazil, Denmark, Greece, Peru, South Africa, Thailand and Sweden. In addition the type was built under licence by SABCA in Belgium and by the Royal Thai Aeronautical Service.

In 1926 Canadian Vickers, who converted a number of RCAF 504Ks to 504N standard, produced a single float 504N seaplane powered by a 200 hp Wright Whirlwind J-4.

The Royal Hellenic Naval Air Force received six Avro 504Os in 1925. The designation 504O was applied to the standard dorsal finned seaplane version of Avro 504N. Other 504Os went to the naval air services of Brazil and Chile while one went to Japan.

The Avro 504Q was a three-seat 160 hp Armstrong Siddeley Lynx powered seaplane built at Hamble in 1924 for that summer's Oxford University Arctic Expedition. After being test flown by Avro test pilot H.J. Hinkler, the machine was shipped to Spitsbergen where it was flown, not without incident, by A.G.B. Ellis and J.C.C. Taylor. On 8 August, the machine reached a record 80° 15'N. It was later abandoned at Spitsbergen.

First flown with a 100 hp Gnome Monosoupape in June 1926, G-EBNE, the Hamble-built Avro 504R Gosport prototype, was later experimentally fitted with a 140 hp Armstrong Siddeley Genet Major IA. The Avro 504R was a reworked lightweight development of the basic 504 with tapered ailerons and steerable tailskid. With lower power, the type produced a performance equal to that of the 130 hp Clerget-powered 504K

Ten Gosports were built for the Argentine Military Air Service in 1927 while a further hundred were built under licence at Cordoba. 150 hp Armstrong Siddeley Mongoose powered Gosports were supplied to Estonia and Peru while one went to the RAF.

Section Four

BETWEEN THE

WARS (1919–39) –

NEW TYPES

The first new Avro design to appear after the armistice was the 35 hp Green powered type
534 Baby. The prototype crashed shortly after take off on its first flight on 30 April 1919,
but the second machine, K-131/G-EACQ, achieved success in the 1919 Aerial Derby and
the Victory Trophy Race at Hendon. H.J. Hinkler acquired the machine in 1920 and flew
it to Turin. He later had it shipped to Australia where it is still preserved.

The Avro 534A Water Baby G-EAPS at Hamble in November 1919. There were three further landplane versions of the Baby: the 534B G-EAUG, which had a shorter bottom wing, the clipped wing 534C racer G-EAXL, and the tropicalised 534D, G-EAYM, which went to India. H.A. Hammersley won the 1920 Aerial Derby in the 534B.

H.J. Hinkler, left, with H.G. Leigh who conducted experiments with the multiple wing 'venetian blind' Baby at Hamble in December 1920.

Built for the Avro Transport Company in 1919, the 150 hp Bentley BR.1 powered Avro 536 was an Avro 504K with the width of its fuselage increased by 9 in to allow four passengers to be carried, side by side, in the rear cockpit. Nine of these joyriding machines were built at Hamble while twelve were built in Manchester.

The Avro 536 prototype K-114/G-EACC at Hamble on 25 April 1919. Left to right are R.J. Parrott, Avro's Hamble manager, H.A. Hammersley, the pilot, the Lord Chancellor, Lord Birkenhead, with his son who had just flown in the machine, and Cdr. Chillcott.

The Avro 536 prototype G-EACC, after conversion to become the sole Avro 536 seaplane, leaving Hamble for the Isle of Wight in August 1919. Standard Avro Transport Company 536s were stationed at Hounslow Heath, Southsea, Weston-Super-Mare, Margate and Blackpool where 500 passengers flew in them on the first day of flying.

The Avro 538 K-132/G-EACR at Southport in 1919. The 150 hp Bentley BR.1 powered machine was used solely by J.C.C. Taylor, the Chief Engineer of the Avro Transport Company, to commute between joyriding sites. Developed from the Avro 531 Spider, the 538 was intended as a racer but was restricted to straight and level flight by a main spar defect.

The Avro 539 at its first launch at Hamble in August 1919. The seaplane, in 539A form with modified rudder, was the reserve aircraft for the 1919 Schneider Trophy Race.

Avro pilot Capt. D.G. Westgarth-Heslam with the type 539A after it had been rebuilt to take a 450 hp Napier Lion as the Avro 539B. He was at the controls when it overran on landing after its first flight and was destroyed at Hamble on 13 July 1921, three days before the Aerial Derby. After the 1919 Schneider Trophy Race, which was cancelled because of fog, the 240 hp Siddeley Puma powered 539A was converted to a landplane. In this form the machine was flown by Westgarth-Heslam in the 1920 Aerial Derby, but he was forced to land drenched in fuel at Abridge, Essex.

The Avro 540 was a gunnery trainer version of the Avro 504K with a rear cockpit scarff ring gun mount. There were only a few such conversions.

Following the downturn in business after the end of the First World War, A.V. Roe and Co. Ltd sought to diversify into the motor car business. Conceived in 1919, only a few 10 hp Avro cars were built at Newton Heath in 1920 before Crossley Motors Ltd took a controlling interest in the firm and production was halted.

The two-seat Avro 543 Baby with its original 35 hp Green engine. The machine was entered in the 1921 Aerial Derby and the 1922 and 1923 King's Cup Races but forced landed in each. The Green was replaced by a 60 hp ADC Cirrus I at Shoreham during 1926, and the machine remained airworthy until 1932.

The Avro 504K G-EAPR was experimentally fitted with a 90 hp Curtiss OX-5 in October 1919 and given the designation Avro 545. The eight-cylinder water-cooled engine required large radiators either side of the fuselage, giving a significant weight penalty.

Built at Hamble along with the Avro 536s in 1919, the Bentley BR.1 powered Avro 546 had a cabin for three passengers in a widened fuselage. It was registered G-EAOM but despite being issued with a certificate of airworthiness in December 1919, it made only a few flights from Hamble and Brighton and was withdrawn from use in 1920.

The Avro 547 four-passenger triplane at the second Aerial Derby at Victoria Park Racecourse, Sydney, on 6 May 1922. The 160 hp Beardmore powered machine, built at Hamble in early 1920, was acquired by QANTAS in November 1920. After a short, troubled, career its airworthiness certificate was withdrawn, a major blow to its owners.

A.V. Roe and H.A. Hammersley, right, with the 240 hp Siddeley Puma engined Avro 547A G-EAUJ at Hamble. The machine was displayed at the Olympia Aero Show in July 1920. The following month it went to Martlesham for the Air Ministry Competition where it was considered to be unstable during comparative trials with other machines.

The 80 hp Renault powered Avro 548 was a 504K modified to carry two passengers in tandem behind the pilot, and had a distinctive centre-section fuel tank. A.V. Roe made only a small number of 548 conversions with others being produced by The Aircraft Disposal Co., by three private operators, and by companies in Australia and Canada.

When fitted with the 120 hp Airdisco engine, the Avro 548 was redesignated 548A. There were four such machines: G-EBKN, converted by the Aircraft Disposal Co., and three assembled by A.V. Roe for the North Sea Aerial and General Transport Co.

J6852, the first of two prototype Avro 549 Aldershot heavy bombers at Hamble in its original form with dorsal fin and short fuselage. First flown by H.J. Hinkler in early 1922, it was modified before being displayed at the Hendon RAF display that June.

J6852, which initially flew with a 650 hp Rolls-Royce Condor III, was later fitted with a 1,000 hp Napier Cub engine and four-wheeled undercarriage to become the Aldershot II. It was first flown in this form by Hinkler at Hamble on 15 December 1922 in front of A.V. Roe and VIPs from the Air Ministry and the engine manufacturers.

Fifteen Avro 549C Aldershot IIIs with 650 hp Rolls-Royce Condor engines were built for the RAF. The machines, which could carry a 2,000 lb bomb load and were armed with a Lewis gun, equipped No. 99 Squadron at Bircham Newton, Norfolk, from August 1924 to December 1925.

The Avro 552 was conceived as a high-power advanced trainer development of the Avro 504K that made use of surplus 180 hp Wolseley Viper water-cooled engines. Avro's test machine G-EAPR was reconfigured as the Avro 552 seaplane only after having first flown as the Avro 552A with wheeled undercarriage. Thirteen Avro 552 seaplanes were built for the Argentine Navy and at least two went to Bulgaria.

G-EAPR in Avro 552A form with 504K undercarriage, which was replaced by a V-type unit for the 1921 Aerial Derby. L.R. Tait-Cox flew it into fifth place. Five Avro 552As were built in Canada and three were assembled from spares in Surrey by C.B. Field in 1932.

One of the nine Avro 552 seaplanes built by Canadian Vickers Ltd in 1925 under construction in the company's Montreal factory. The machines served with the Royal Canadian Air Force in the forestry patrol role and had large 25 gallon wing fuel tanks.

The Canadian-built Avro 552 seaplanes had large central wooden floats designed by the US Naval Aircraft Factory. The RCAF Avro 552 and 552As had a short service life, having all been withdrawn from use by September 1928.

G-EAPR was temporarily fitted with a single float undercarriage under the designation Avro 552B to test the configuration used in the Canadian-built Avro 552s.

The ultimate development of the Avro Baby was the 80 hp Le Rhône powered type 554 Antarctic Baby. Built for the 1921 Shackleton-Rowett South Polar Expedition, the machine was not used, as engine trouble in Shackleton's ship *The Quest* resulted in it not calling at Cape Town where essential parts for the Baby were awaiting collection.

The Avro 554 Antarctic Baby being hoisted aboard a sealer in the Canadian Arctic. After some test flying on its return from the Antarctic, the Avro 554 was shipped to Canada in 1923 where Bowring Brothers used it for seal spotting until 1927.

The prototype 450 hp Napier Lion powered Avro 555 Bison carrier-borne naval reconnaissance and fleet gunnery aircraft. Three prototypes were followed by twelve production Bison Is, based on the second prototype with raised top wing and other modifications, which were built at Manchester to Air Ministry order in 1922.

One of the forty-four production Avro 552A Bison IIs at Hamble. Also built at Manchester, the Bison IIs had dorsal fins, no forward portholes, and other modifications. They served with the RAF on coastal patrol duties and with Naval Spotter flights at Gosport and Malta, and on board the carriers HMS *Furious* and HMS *Eagle* until 1929.

The sole Avro 552B Bison I amphibian N9594. Converted from a standard Bison I at Hamble, the machine went to Felixstowe in 1924, where trials were abandoned after it proved to be unstable in flight and to have poor on-water characteristics.

The Avro 557 Ava prototype flying at the 1927 Hendon RAF Display. The twin 650 hp Rolls-Royce Condor III powered machine, which was intended for use in the coastal defence role, was built at Hamble in 1924 but did not appear in public until the RAF Display in July 1926. The Ava could carry a 2,000 lb bomb load or a single torpedo.

The second of the two Avas in the New Types Park at Hendon in July 1927. It differed from the first in being of metal construction and having square cut wingtips. The vehicle in the foreground is the 1926 Avro Monocar which A.V. Roe hoped would bring personal transport to the masses. Only one was built, which A.V. Roe drove extensively.

Two examples of the ultralight single-seat Avro 558 were built for the Lympne trials of October 1923, where H.A. Hammersley won the £100 Duke of Sutherland's prize after reaching a height of 13,850 ft in G-EBHW. This aircraft, which had a 500 cc Douglas motorcycle engine, was flown with a raised undercarriage at the Royal Aero Club Light Plane Demonstration at Hendon in October 1923.

The Avro test pilot H.J. 'Bert' Hinkler in the cockpit of No. 5. This Avro 558 differed from No. 11/G-EBHW in having a B. and H. engine which gave trouble, preventing Hinkler completing any laps of the 12½ mile Lympne Trials circuit. After the competition No. 5 was fitted with a V-type undercarriage and a 698 cc Blackburne Thrush engine.

H.J. Hinkler with the Avro 560 ultralight monoplane at Lympne. Built at Hamble along with the Avro 558s for the 1923 Lympne Trials, the Avro 560 (No. 6) was fitted with an upright 698 cc Blackburne Tomtit engine and successfully completed some eighty laps of the trials circuit. In 1924, powered by an inverted Tomtit, the machine went to Martlesham to be assessed against the Parnall Pixie II and DH.53 Humming Bird.

J7261, the first of three Avro 561 Andover transport/ambulance aircraft built for the RAF, at the Hendon RAF Display on 28 June 1924. Powered by one 650 hp Rolls-Royce Condor III, the machine could carry twelve passengers. All three were based at Halton.

G-EBKW, the sole Avro 563 Andover, taking off from Hamble. This twelve-passenger airliner version of the type 561 was loaned to Imperial Airways for proving flights during 1925. Unlike the military machines, the civil Andover had a toilet and luggage space at the rear. In 1927 it was taken on RAF charge and joined the other Andovers at Halton.

The two-seat Avro 561 Avis was built for the 1924 Lympne Trials. However, at these its 32 hp geared Bristol Cherub gave trouble and the engine was converted overnight to direct drive. Hinkler then beat twelve other aircraft to win the Grosvenor Challenge Trophy. The Avis was tested at Martlesham in 1925 and was at the 1926 Lympne trials.

The Avro 566 Avenger I single-seat fighter was powered by a 525 hp Napier Lion VIII. First flown at Hamble by Hinkler on 26 June 1926, it went to Hendon for the RAF Display on 3 July. The type, which could reach 180 mph, was not selected for the RAF.

In May 1928, a number of modifications were made to G-EBND, including the fitting of smaller mainplanes with ailerons on all four wings and a new 553 hp Napier Lion IX engine. In this form it became the Avro 567 Avenger II, and with the racing No. 32 it was flown in the King's Cup Race on 20 July 1928, winning the prize for fastest time.

The Avro 571 Buffalo I, which was first flown at Hamble in 1926, was a private venture carrier-borne torpedo bomber armed with one forward-firing Vickers gun and two Lewis guns mounted on a scarff ring in the rear cockpit, at the base of which was a prone bombing position for the gunner/wireless operator. After competitive trials at Martlesham, the Blackburn Ripon was selected to meet the fleet requirement.

After the Martlesham trials, the Buffalo was modified at Hamble in 1927 to become the Avro 572 Buffalo II with new metal square cut wings, a 530 hp Napier Lion XIA, and other features designed to improve performance and general handling.

The inside of the Avro factory at Hamble in the summer of 1928. In the centre is the Buffalo II after acquisition by the Air Ministry and conversion to a seaplane. In this form it went to the Marine Aircraft Experimental Establishment at Felixstowe who used it for trials and as a hack after it was found to be 'unsuitable for production'.

F.T. Courtney flying the 130 hp Clerget powered Avro 574 autogiro at Hamble in June 1926. After the same pilot had convincingly demonstrated the Cierva-built C.6A, the Air Ministry ordered two similar but higher powered Avro 504K fuselaged machines from A.V. Roe. These were the Avro 574, or Cierva C.6C, and the Avro 587, or Cierva C.6D.

The Avro 575, or Cierva C.8L Mk.I, autogiro was based on a standard Avro 504N fuselage with a 180 hp Armstrong Siddeley Lynx engine. The machine, built to an Air Ministry order, was first flown at Hamble by H.J. Hinkler in 1927. It was based at Farnborough until 1930 when it was damaged beyond repair in a crash.

Continuing the association with the Cierva Autogiro Co., the Avro 576, or Cierva C.9, was powered by a 70 hp Armstrong Siddeley Genet and had a fuselage of entirely new design. Hinkler first flew the single-seat machine at Hamble in September 1927 while a year later at Farnborough it was fitted with half-length untapered rotor blades.

The Avro 581 Avian, which employed a two-seat version of the Avro 576 autogiro fuselage, was built for the 1926 Lympne Light Aeroplane trials. Numbered 9, it performed well in the trials, until eliminated when magneto problems resulted in a forced landing near Lewes. Success, however, later came in a race round the trials circuit.

Bert Hinkler with the Avian prototype which he bought after it had been re-engined with an 85 hp ADC Cirrus II and fitted with new larger fin and rudder to become the Avro 581A. Hinkler flew it with success at the 1927 Bournemouth Easter Meeting and that August, equipped with a long range tank, he flew non-stop to Riga, Latvia in $10^{3}/_{4}$ hours.

Hinkler arriving at Karachi during his flight from Croydon to Australia in 1928. Equipped with the wings from the type 594C Avian and metal propeller, in which form it became the Avro 581E, Hinkler departed from Croydon on 7 February and arrived at Darwin fifteen days later after having flown more than 11,000 miles in 128 hours flying time. The machine is still preserved in the Brisbane Museum, Queensland.

In March 1926, Avro's experimental 504N G-EBKQ was fitted with RAF 30 section mainplanes, an arrangement that was given the type number 582. H.A. Hammersley raced the Avro 582 at the Bournemouth Easter Meeting in April 1927.

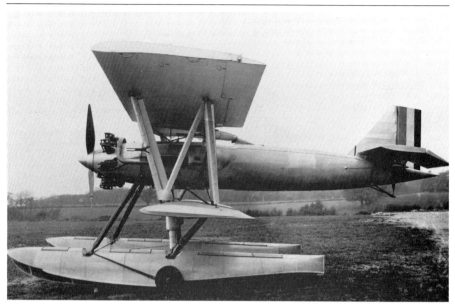

The Avro 584 Avocet was a single-seat naval fighter powered by a 180 hp Armstrong Siddeley Lynx IV. It could be fitted with wheeled undercarriage for carrier operations or floats for catapulting from a cruiser. Armament was two forward-firing Vickers guns.

N210, the second of the two Avocet prototypes, differed from the first, N209, in having larger vertical tail surfaces. The type's performance was unspectacular and no production order was forthcoming. After both machines had been assessed at Martlesham in February 1929, N210 was fitted with floats and served as a practice machine for Schneider Trophy pilots at the RAF High Speed Flight's base at Calshot.

The fourth 100 hp Avro Alpha powered Avro 504R Gosport G-EBPH was fitted with a 504N-type undercarriage in late 1926 to become the Avro 585. The modification was made to facilitate a landing on the 3,118 ft summit of Helvellyn in Cumbria, a feat achieved by Hinkler, with J.F. Leeming as passenger, on 22 December 1926. The Avro Alpha engine was built in small numbers by Crossley Motors.

The Avro 587, or Cierva C.6D, was the first ever two-seat autogiro. It was first flown by F.T. Courtney at Hamble on 29 July 1926 with Don Juan de la Cierva himself becoming the first ever passenger to fly in a rotary wing aircraft the following day.

The Avro 587, after registration as G-EBTW and conversion to Cierva C.8R standard with stub wings and tapered rotor blades, flying behind the Avro 586 (Cierva C.8V). This latter machine, G-EBTX, used the fuselage and powerplant of the Avro 552A G-EAPR. It was demonstrated by Hinkler at Croydon on 20 0ctober 1927 but the machine reverted to being an Avro 552A after a rebuild in 1930.

The Avro 586 (Cierva C.8V), left, with the Avro 574 (Cierva C.6C) J8068 in January 1927. The former has the experimental four-wheel undercarriage, while the latter has the modified stub wings with ailerons which were fitted shortly before it crashed.

The 85 hp ADC Cirrus II powered production version of the Avian was the type 594. There were two Avian Is, G-EBQL, flown by Dudley Watt in the 1927 King's Cup Race, and G-EBQN, built for the Royal Aircraft Establishment Aero Club at Farnborough.

Mrs S.C. Elliott-Lynn with her Avro 594 Avian II G-EBRS, the third of the nine built. Mrs Elliott-Lynn, later Lady Heath, did much to promote the type. On 19 July 1927 she flew 1,200 miles round England, making some seventy-nine landings; shortly afterwards she flew to Poland and back, and that August attended the Zurich International Meeting.

The Avro Alpha engined type 594A Avian II G-EBSD as the type 594C, with the special mainplanes with which it was flown to a record height (for a light aircraft with a passenger) of 19,200 ft, by Mrs Elliott-Lynn on 8 October 1927. Initially a single seater, 'SD was converted to a two seater for the record attempt.

Capt. W.N. 'Bill' Lancaster and Mrs Keith Miller with the Avro 594 Avian III G-EBTU *Red Rose* during a break in their flight to Australia. They left Croydon on 14 October 1927 but were dogged by bad luck and did not arrive at Darwin until 19 March 1928. *Red Rose* remained in Australia, was re-registered VH-UTU, and survived until 1936.

Flt. Lt. Patrick Murdoch of the South African Air Force with the Avian III G-EBVU *John*, which he flew from Croydon to Cape Town in a record fifteen days between 29 July and 12 August 1928. The machine was destroyed and Flt. Lt. Murdoch injured when it crashed near Elizabethville in the Belgian Congo during the return flight to Croydon.

NC367, one of seventeen production Avian IIIs that were imported into the USA by Air Associates Inc. of New York. The improved Avian IV also went to the USA in significant numbers with Air Associates acquiring eleven and the Whittlesey Body Company thirty-four.

Miss Winifred Brown holding the prestigious King's Cup after winning the 1930 race in the Avian III G-EBVZ, the first woman to do so. She also became the first pilot ever to win the King's Cup and the Siddeley Challenge Trophy for light aeroplane club entrants in the same year. Holding the Siddeley Trophy is V.R. Adams, her fiancé and navigator.

The two 80 hp Armstrong Siddeley Genet II powered Avro 594B Avian IVs used by the Ottawa Flying Club in Canada. With club officials is W.L. McIntyre (second from left), General Manager of the Ottawa Car Co., which later assembled Avro 616 Avian IVMs.

N38, later LN-ABF, which was delivered to Norway by Alf Gunnerstad in June 1929, was used by the Norwegian Antarctic Expedition of 1933–4. Other export Avian IVMs went to Argentina, Australia, Brazil, Mexico, South Africa and Spain.

The Avro 604 Antelope high performance day bomber was first flown at Hamble in November 1927. The 480 hp Rolls-Royce F.XIB powered machine was unsuccessful in competitive trials at Martlesham in September 1928 and there was no production order. The machine was later used as a test bed for variable pitch propellers at Farnborough.

Avro type number 605 was allotted to the Avian IIIA seaplane. G.H. Storck left Hamble in his Avro 605 NX6633 for an intended 27,000 mile round the world flight on 15 September 1928 but the machine overturned on take-off from Corsica a week later.

The 180 hp Armstrong Siddeley Lynx IV powered Avro 611, or Cierva C.8L Mk.II, was built to the order of J.G. Weir, Chairman of the Cierva Autogiro Co. The machine, with Cierva at the controls, became the first rotary wing aircraft to cross the English Channel on 18 September 1928. It is preserved in the Musée de l'Air at Le Bourget, Paris.

The Avro 612, or Cierva C.17, autogiro was based on the Avian IIIA and had a 90 hp ADC Cirrus III engine. It was first flown by Juan de la Cierva on 23 October 1928, but the machine was underpowered and it was subsequently dismantled.

The Avro 616 Avian IVM differed from the early wooden type 594 Avian IV in having a steel-tube fuselage. The type was built in significant numbers by A.V. Roe and others were assembled in Canada by the Ottawa Car Co. and in the USA by the Whittlesey Body Co. A number of different engines were fitted to the basic Avian IVM airframe.

No. 133, one of the ten 135 hp Genet Major I powered Avian IVMs erected in Canada for the Royal Canadian Air Force in 1929 using fuselages supplied by A.V. Roe. Ten machines were also supplied to flying clubs, which later also received some former RCAF machines, including Avro-built examples. The RCAF made little use of their Avian IVMs.

H.F. 'Jim' Broadbent flying his Sports Avian VH-UQE, in which he made a record one-day solo flight round four Australian states on 12 August 1931 and completed a record flight of 7,600 miles round Australia the following month. The improved performance model was powered by a 105 hp ADC Cirrus Hermes I and sixteen were built.

VH-UQG Southern Cross Minor was the second of two single-seat 120 hp de Havilland Gipsy II engined long-range Avian Vs built for Sir Charles Kingsford Smith. On 21 September 1931 the owner left Melbourne for England in 'QG but his record attempt ended in Turkey owing to illness. The machine was sold to W.N. Lancaster, who perished in the Sahara after crashing during an attempt on the Cape Town record in April 1933. His body and the wrecked Avian lay undiscovered until March 1962.

The Avro 617, or Cierva C.8L Mk.III, autogiro was built for the Italian Government. The 180 hp Armstrong Siddeley Lynx IV powered machine was test flown by A.H. Rawson in September 1928.

Fourteen Avro 618 Ten 240 hp Armstrong Siddeley Lynx IV powered anglicised versions of the successful Fokker F.VIIb/3m airliner were built under licence between 1929 and 1936. Five were supplied to Australian National Airways, including VH-UNA, which crashed in Malaya while en route to Croydon carrying the 1931 Christmas mail.

The Avro 619 Five was a scaled down 105 hp Armstrong Siddeley Genet Major powered version of the Avro Ten. Four aircraft were built, two for Wilson Airways in Kenya (which were later joined by the Avro demonstrator) and one machine which was based in Brisbane with the Queensland Air Navigation Co., the operator of two Avro Tens.

The 100 hp Alpha engined autogiro, a modified version of the Avro 620, or Cierva C.17 Mk. II, G-AAGJ, flying at Hamble. The Avian III-based machine was later fitted with twin floats to become the Hydrogiro, in which form it was flown by Don Juan de la Cierva from Southampton Water on 25 April 1930.

The 215 hp Armstrong Siddeley Lynx IVC powered Avro 621 Tutor was adopted as the standard RAF trainer in June 1932, and some 381 were built for the service.

No. 740, one of fifty-seven Avro 621s built in South Africa for the South African Air Force. Three examples were also constructed under licence in Denmark. Avro-built 621s, the name Tutor only applied to the RAF version, were also supplied to civil operators while military models went to Canada, China, Denmark, Greece, Poland and South Africa.

Avro Tutor production at Newton Heath in 1935. A total of 795 Avro 621s were built, including eleven Avro 621 Trainers (155 hp Armstrong Siddeley Mongoose IIIC) for the RAF.

One prototype and fourteen production Sea Tutors were built for the Air Ministry under the designation Avro 646. They were delivered between 1934 and 1936 and used for trials at the Marine Aircraft Experimental Establishment at Felixstowe, and for instruction at the Seaplane Training School at Calshot until April 1938.

The Avro 624 Six prototype G-AAYR with the Avro class B registration K-5. This slightly larger version of the Avro Five had a widened two-seat cockpit, dual controls, a lavatory and other improvements. Of the three aircraft built, two, including G-AAYR, went to China while the third, in modified form, saw service with Air Service Training at Hamble.

G-AAYV, the first of two Avro 625 Avian Monoplanes was powered by a 100 hp Armstrong Siddeley Genet Major. Wearing the racing number 84, it was flown by F. Tomkins in the 1930 King's Cup Race but retired because of unfavourable handicapping. The machine was later rebuilt as a standard Avian IVM biplane.

The second Avro 652 Avian Monoplane G-AAYW differed from the first in having a 105 hp Cirrus Hermes I. Flown by T. Neville Stack, it came 48th in the 1930 King's Cup. The aircraft was sold to Flt. Lt. R.L.R. Atcherley who flew it to Iraq when posted there in 1932. From 1939 it was based at Birmingham with a new owner and flew till 1940.

An Avro 626 of the Estonian Air Force. The 626 was developed from the type 621 to meet the requirements of overseas air arms. Conversion kits enabled the aircraft to be configured for a variety of training roles and there was provision for a gunner in the enlarged rear cockpit. There was large scale production for several foreign governments.

An Avro 626 Prefect of the Royal New Zealand Air Force. The 260 hp Armstrong Siddeley Cheetah V powered Prefect was a specialist navigational trainer. Seven Prefects, without gunner's position, were supplied to the RAF in 1935, replacing the Avro 621 Trainers at the School of Air Navigation at Andover, while four machines with the gunner's position went to New Zealand, also in 1935.

The Avro 627 Mailplane under construction at Newton Heath in 1931. In 1928 work began on the Avro 608 Hawk G-EBWM but this private venture fighter was not completed and the airframe was redesigned first as the Avro 622 and eventually still further to take the 525 hp Armstrong Siddeley Panther IIA as the type 627 Mailplane.

The Avro 627 was designed to meet a possible Canadian Airways requirement for a mailplane. It was demonstrated at Heston on 10 August 1931 and then shipped to Canada, but the untimely withdrawal of local subsidies meant there were no orders. In 1932 the Mailplane was flown in the King's Cup by H.A. Brown, Avro's chief test pilot.

In June 1933 the Mailplane was modified to become the Avro 654 high performance test bed powered by a 700 hp Armstrong Siddeley Tiger IV. Initially it was a single seater but an observer's seat was later provided in the original mail compartment. The machine had a short service life and was dismantled in 1934.

The 135 hp Armstrong Siddeley Genet Major I powered Avro 631 Cadet was a trainer primarily for club use. Air Service Training Ltd at Hamble operated a fleet of seventeen while the Irish Air Corps received seven, four went to Hong Kong and single examples to Brazil, China and Portugal. Maj. J.E.D. Shaw's G-ABVV was the only private Cadet.

The Avro 636 was a two-seat fighter trainer. Only four aircraft were completed, all to the order of the Irish Army Air Corps, and these were delivered in August 1935. They were powered by 460 hp Armstrong Siddeley Jaguar IVCs, and though the type number 667 was allocated to this variant they were always referred to as 636s.

Eight Avro 637 frontier patrol aircraft developed from the type 626 were supplied to the Kwangsi Air Force in China in 1933–4. The rear gunner was provided with a Lewis Gun, it could carry up to six 20 lb bombs and the rear decking could be hinged back so that a stretcher case could be carried if required. It also had a large fuel tank.

The Avro 638 Club Cadet G-ACIL was unique in having a 140 hp Cirrus Hermes IVA. The type was essentially a folding wing version of the Avro 631 Cadet and the standard powerplant was, as in the 631, the 135 hp Armstrong Siddeley Genet Major I. Some sixteen were completed and the main users were Airwork and the Southend Flying Club.

G-ACGA was the sole Avro 639 Cabin Cadet. It was flown initially in 1933 with the class B marks K-14 (the letter K being allocated to Avro) and was withdrawn from use in 1934. The Genet Major powered machine could carry two passengers, who sat side by side behind the pilot, but it was never granted a certificate of airworthiness.

Nine Avro 640 Cadet three seaters with provision for two passengers sitting side by side in a widened front cockpit, were built. Of these four, including G-ACFU, built for the Scottish Motor Traction Co. had 140 hp Cirrus Hermes IV engines and the remainder Genet Major Is. Three, one painted red, one white and one blue, were employed by Sir Alan Cobham's National Aviation Day Displays for joyriding and parachute dropping.

The Avro 641 Commodore was a four/five-seat air taxi or private touring aircraft powered by a 215 hp Armstrong Siddeley Lynx IVC which was fitted with an electric starter. Six Commodores were built in 1934, including one for the Maharajah of Vizianagram. Two, sold to Egypt in 1936, later served with the Egyptian Air Force.

The Avro 642/2m under construction at Newton Heath in 1933 showing the original rounded nose. The 460 hp Armstrong Siddeley Jaguar VID powered machine, which was known initially as the Avro Eighteen, could carry sixteen passengers and two crew.

After being damaged in a gale not long after completion, the nose of the Avro 642/2m was changed to a more conventional design. The machine was delivered to Midland and Scottish Air Ferries at Glasgow in April 1934, but moved south to Croydon when acquired by Commercial Air Hire in May 1935. In June 1936 the 642/2m went to New Guinea where it was used for mail services until destroyed by the Japanese in 1942.

The four-engined version of the Avro 642 was the type 642/4m and, like the twin-engined version, only one was built. The aircraft was ordered by the Indian Government and served as the personal aircraft of the Viceroy from 1935 until 1940. Named Star of India, it was a seven seater and had 215 hp Armstrong Siddeley Lynx IVC engines.

The Avro 643 Cadet was an improved version of the type 631 with slightly modified fuselage and raised rear seat. Only eight were built, one going to Spain, with the remainder seeing service with clubs and private owners in Britain. Two aircraft flew post-war and both were later sold in Ireland, where they remain in storage.

Avro 643 Mk.II Cadets of the Royal Australian Air Force. Thirty-four of these aircraft, which had the more powerful 150 hp Genet IA, were delivered to the RAAF. In Britain Air Service Training acquired twenty-three while one went to Brazil and two to Malaya.

The Avro 652 twin 270 hp Armstrong Siddeley Cheetah V powered four-seat long-range airliner was designed to meet an Imperial Airways specification. Flown for the first time at Woodford on 7 January 1935, the type was used on the airline's Croydon to Brindisi route. In 1938 both machines became navigation trainers with Air Service Training.

K6316, one of 174 production Avro 652A Anson 1s ordered in 1935. An Air Ministry specification for a twin-engined coastal patrol aircraft was close to that of the Imperial Airways machine. Thus was born the type 652A and the prototype K4771, which was powered by 290 hp Cheetah VIs, was first flown on 24 March 1935 by S.A. 'Bill' Thorn. Before the Second World War around nine hundred Anson Is were built, some going overseas.

The type number Avro 661 was given to a special wing equipped with split flaps designed by the Zap Development Corporation. It was fitted to the Parnall Parasol K1229 and was tested at Farnborough between February and August 1934.

The Avro 671 was a licence-built Cierva C.30A powered by a 140 hp Armstrong Siddeley Genet IA. Twelve were built for the Air Ministry, and fifty-four others mostly for British private owners but a few to foreign civil and military operators. G-ACUU was the last of its breed to fly, being retired in 1960. It is currently preserved at Duxford.

The military version of the Avro 671, which was known as the Rota I, was used for Army co-operation duties. During the Second World War surviving Rota Is and requisitioned civil machines were employed calibrating coastal radar stations. K4296 was the only Rota I fitted with floats and was first flown in this form at Rochester on 15 April 1935.

The Avro 674 was an improved version of the Hawker Audax army co-operation biplane, 287 of which had earlier been built by A.V. Roe for the RAF. Twenty-four Avro 674s were built for the Egyptian Army Air Force during 1937 and 1938. The first six had 750 hp Armstrong Siddeley Panther VIA engines and the remainder Panther Xs.

THE SECOND WORLD WAR (1939–45)

At the outbreak of war, the Avro Anson I was in mass production. The type was briefly used offensively with one machine bombing a U-boat on 5 September 1939 and another shooting down a Dornier Do.18 flying boat later the same month.

Woodford in 1940, showing the hangars then used for final assembly of aircraft built at Newton Heath and Chadderton. Lined up outside are newly completed Ansons and a few of the 1,005 Bristol Blenheims built by A.V. Roe & Co.

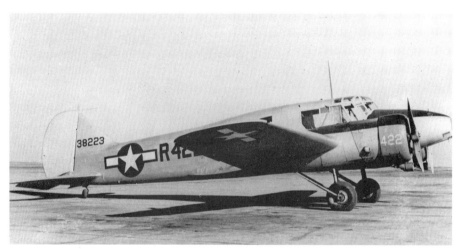

Fifty Canadian-built Anson IIs supplied to the USAAF as advanced crew trainers were known as Federal AT-20s. Canadian-built Ansons equipped the flying schools of the Commonwealth Air Training Plan and some 1,832 were built by Federal Aircraft and five other companies. The Anson II had 330 hp Jacobs L6MB engines and revised windows.

The Canadian-built Avro Anson V had a wooden fuselage in order to save on the use of steel. The prototype, first flown in 1942, was followed by 1,050 production aircraft built by the Canadian Car and Foundry Co. and McDonald Brothers. They were used as navigational trainers and were powered by 450 hp Pratt and Whitney Wasp Juniors. The type remained in service with the RCAF and Royal Canadian Navy until the late 1950s.

No. 13881, the sole Anson VI gunnery trainer version of the Anson V, was built by Federal Aircraft at Montreal. It was first flown at Cartierville, Montreal, on 21 September 1943.

The prototype 1,760 hp Rolls-Royce Vulture I powered Avro 679 Manchester I heavy bomber made its maiden flight at Ringway, Manchester, on 25 July 1939. Production machine L7279/EM-B was delivered to No. 207 Sqdn at Waddington in November 1940 and took part in the type's first operation, a raid on Brest in February 1941. Manchesters later participated in the first 1,000 bomber raid on Cologne on 30 May 1942.

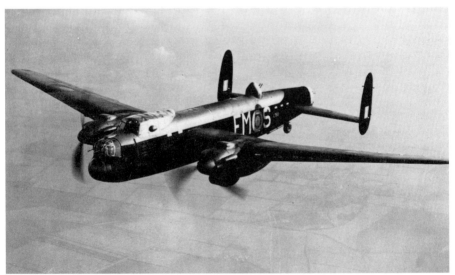

EM-S, a twin fin Manchester IA of No. 207 Sqdn. All Manchester Is were retrospectively fitted with twin fin tail units after they were found to be superior to the triple fin arrangement. 156 Manchesters were built by Avro and forty-four by Metropolitan Vickers, but their engines were unreliable and the type had a short service career.

The Avro 683 Lancaster prototype BT308 with its original Manchester three fin tail unit. Conceived as the Manchester III, BT308 was a standard Manchester fitted with a new centre and outer wing sections to accommodate four 1,145 hp Rolls-Royce Merlin X engines. The machine was first flown on 9 January 1941 and later went to Boscombe Down for trials. It was during these that a larger twin fin Lancaster tail unit was fitted.

Production Avro 683 Lancaster Is could carry a 7,000 lb load and had a range of 2,530 miles. No. 44 Squadron at Waddington was the first to fly the type operationally, in March 1942, while the following month twelve aircraft from two squadrons bombed a diesel engine factory at Augsburg and Sqdn. Ldr. J.D. Nettleton won the Victoria Cross.

Final assembly of Lancaster Is at Sir W.G. Armstrong Whitworth Aircraft's plant at Baginton, Coventry. The company, along with Austin Motors, Metropolitan-Vickers, and Vickers-Armstrong, produced the type in addition to A.V. Roe. Some 7,374 Lancasters were built with production reaching a peak of 293 per month in 1944.

The Lancaster II had 1,650 hp Bristol Hercules VI engines in place of the 1,280 hp Merlins of the Lancaster I. The alternative powerplant was to guard against possible interruption of Merlin supplies, but with Hercules being required for other types and Merlins remaining available, only 300 Lancaster IIs were built, all at Baginton.

Lancaster ED817/AJ-C, with modified undersides, was used for the test dropping off the Kent coast in April 1943 of the bouncing bombs used in the famous Dambusters raid. Nineteen production versions of these special aircraft were used by 617 Squadron in the historic raids on the Möhne and Eder dams which took place on 16 May 1943.

Wing Commander Guy Gibson (in centre with arms folded), who led the Dambusters raid and who was awarded the Victoria Cross, with other pilots of Scampton-based 617 Squadron. In order to launch the bouncing bombs successfully, the Lancasters had to be flown accurately at a height of 60 ft and at a speed of 220 mph.

In Canada Victory Aircraft built 430 Lancaster Xs, which like the British Lancaster III had Merlins built in America by the Packard company. The Lancaster Xs were flown across the Atlantic and served with both RAF and British based RCAF units.

The prototype Avro 685 York transport aircraft in its original form with twin fin tail unit. The Merlin powered machine was first flown at Ringway on 5 July 1942 and the following month it went to Boscombe Down. Following trials there, the Air Ministry ordered three further prototypes and a limited number of production aircraft. The third prototype York LV633 *Ascalon* was used by the Prime Minister, Winston Churchill, and this machine, together with two other VIP Yorks, ferried personnel to allied conferences.

The prototype York after conversion to become the sole York C.Mk. 2 with Bristol Hercules VI engines and the three fin tail unit fitted to all production Yorks. The aircraft first flew in this form on 17 March 1944. It later became an instructional airframe.

In 1944 five Yorks were delivered to BOAC and were used on the airline's flights to Cairo via Morocco, which began on 22 April. Twelve passengers were carried in addition to freight. There were 208 production Yorks and there were passenger, freight and combined passenger/freight versions. All were built at Ringway apart from the last eight which were completed at Yeadon. The last York was rolled out in April 1948.

Trans Canada Air Line's civilianised Lancaster III CF-CMS at Prestwick. It was this machine, the forerunner of the Avro 691 Lancastrian, that inaugurated the Canada-UK air service on 22 July 1943. Victory Aircraft civilianised seven further Lancasters, the last five being Lancaster XPPs which were outwardly similar to the later Lancastrian.

G-AGLF, the first nine-passenger Avro 691 Lancastrian, was delivered to BOAC in early 1945 and two months later was flown to New Zealand in the record time of $3\frac{1}{2}$ days. Twenty-one were supplied to BOAC and the type was used on the Kangaroo service to Australia in association with QANTAS and on services to South America. A total of eighty-two Lancastrians of various marks were built for BOAC, other civil operators and the RAF.

Section Six

POST WAR (1945–62)

Anson and Tudor production at Woodford in 1947. At the head of the Anson line are

metal-winged Anson Mk.18s for the Royal Afghan Air Force. Thirteen Mk.18s for general

purpose and police duties went to Afghanistan while a further twelve Mk.18C specialist

aircrew trainers were built for the Indian Government.

G-AGPG, the first production Avro 19 series 1, was built in 1945 and remained in service with A.V. Roe & Co. until 1961. This Anson variant was a nine-seat feed-liner, the main civil user of which was Railway Air Services, which acquired fourteen. Others saw service with independent charter companies. The military version, the Anson C.Mk.19 series 1, was built in numbers for the RAF as a general transport.

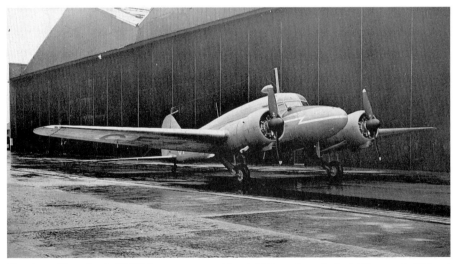

The Avro 19 series 2 CF-FEQ was operated by A.V. Roe Canada Ltd. The mark differed from the series 1 in having tapered wings. 158 Anson C.Mk.19 series 2 were delivered to the RAF while fourteen Avro 19 series 2s were built for civil and overseas customers.

VM306, the prototype of the final version of the Anson, the T.Mk.22 radio trainer, first flew in June 1948. In all, 11,020 Ansons were built, the last of which, a T.Mk.21 navigational trainer, was test flown by Avro's Chief Test Pilot J.H. Orrell on 15 May 1952 and was later handed over to the RAF by Managing Director Sir Roy Dobson.

The civilianised Lancaster G-AGJI was delivered to the BOAC Development Flight at Hurn in January 1944 and was used for developing equipment for post-war transport aircraft. It later served as a testbed for the 1,750 hp Rolls-Royce Merlin 102 engine which was used in the Avro 688 Tudor I.

In Canada the Lancaster X FM209 served as testbed for the Avro Orenda turbojet, later used in the Avro Canada CF-100, while another was used to test the 3,000 lb thrust Avro Chinook TR.4 Mk.II. In Britain ten Lancasters served as testbeds for a variety of piston, turbine and turbojet engines while a further Lancaster testbed flew in Sweden.

One of the last users of the Lancaster was the Royal Canadian Air Force, which withdrew its last three machines from service on 1 April 1964. The French Navy also used Lancasters into the 1960s. One B.Mk.VII, which saw service in New Caledonia, was flown back to Britain in 1965 and is still preserved at East Kirkby, Lincolnshire.

British South American Airways acquired twelve Yorks in 1946 while four others went to FAMA in Argentina. Independent airlines, most notably Skyways, which had earlier acquired three new machines, continued to operate former BOAC and military Yorks throughout the 1950s. The last York, owned by Dan-Air, was withdrawn in 1963.

The first production twelve-passenger Avro 688 Tudor I with its original tail unit. The Merlin powered Tudor was the first British pressurised airliner. In 1947, two years after the prototype first flew, BOAC rejected the type as being incapable of transatlantic operation. Two aircraft were later converted into Tudor 3 VIP aircraft for ministerial use while a further three were used as freighters during the Berlin Air Lift of 1948–9.

The Avro 688 Tudor 4 was a modified Tudor I with a 6 ft fuselage extension to meet British South American Airways requirements. Five of the aircraft, which could carry thirty-two passengers plus cargo, were built for BSAA. They were used on the airline's London to Bermuda route together with two twenty-eight passenger Tudor 4Bs converted from Tudor 1s.

In 1956, Aviation Traders at Southend, which had acquired all remaining Tudors three years earlier, installed a large freight door into six machines and renamed them Avro Super Traders. Air Charter successfully flew them on long-range charters until 1959. Super Trader 4B G-AGRH, which started life as a Tudor I and was used on the Berlin Air Lift, crashed into Mt. Suphan Dag, Turkey, in April 1959 while en route to Australia.

The second prototype Tudor I G-AGST was converted to a Tudor 4 and later fitted with twin 5,000 lb st Rolls-Royce Nene 5 turbojets to become the sole Tudor 8. In this form it flew in military markings, and after demonstration by J.H. Orrell at the 1948 Farnborough Show it went to Boscombe Down for trials. It was broken up at Farnborough in 1951.

The Avro 689 Tudor 2 was a sixty-passenger stretched and widened version of the type 688 Tudor I. It had been selected as standard equipment for BOAC, QANTAS and South African Airways but an order for seventy-nine was reduced after teething troubles forced modifications, including the fitting of the distinctive large tail, which added weight and reduced performance. All orders were later cancelled when the prototype crashed.

Avro personalities after the first flight of the Tudor 2 prototype G-AGSU on 10 March 1946. From left to right on the steps are test pilot J.H. Orrell, the legendary Chief Designer Roy Chadwick, Flight Engineer Bowers and the Director of Production C.E. Fielding, while in the foreground is the Chief Test Pilot S.A. 'Bill' Thorn. Roy Chadwick and Bill Thorn were among those killed when 'SU crashed at Woodford on 23 August 1947.

Six Avro 689 Tudor 5s, identified by circular windows, were built as 44-passenger airliners for BSAA. They did not go into service and all, including one sold to Airflight, were used instead as tankers on the Berlin Air Lift. For a few years after this, several were used by charter companies, most notably for tourist flights to Johannesburg.

In an attempt to improve the type's performance, the first production Tudor 2 G-AGRX was completed as the sole Tudor 7 with 1,750 hp Bristol Hercules 120s in place of the standard Merlins. It first flew on 17 April 1946 and was displayed at the 1946 Radlett Show. It was later used by the Telecommunications Research Establishment at Defford.

Avro 691 Lancastrians, including some former military machines, saw service with BSAA and civil operators such as Skyways and Silver City Airways until the early 1950s. Five former BSAA/BOAC machines, equipped by Flight Refuelling Ltd with 2,500 gallon fuselage tanks, were used to ship petrol and diesel to Berlin during the Air Lift.

VL970 was one of two Lancastrians used by Rolls-Royce to test the Rolls-Royce Avon turbojet. In total nine Lancastrians were used as engine testbeds, and among other powerplants flight tested were the Rolls-Royce Nene, the De Havilland Ghost, the Rolls-Royce Griffon 57 and the Armstrong Siddeley Sapphire.

The prototype Avro 694 Lincoln was first flown at Ringway by Capt. H.A. Brown on 9 June 1944. The type, which was powered by 1,750 hp Rolls-Royce Merlins, was conceived as an improved Lancaster for the war against Japan. Lincolns, however, did not enter service until after the war had ended and production orders were cut back.

Twenty squadrons were equipped with Lincolns. The type, which was the RAF's last piston-engined bomber, was used operationally against terrorists in Malaya and Kenya but had been completely withdrawn from front line duties by 1955. The last five, used by 151 Squadron, Signals Command, at Watton, were withdrawn from use in 1963.

Eighteen Royal Australian Air Force Lincolns were fitted with lengthened noses to accommodate anti-submarine radar and redesignated Lincoln Mk.31(MR)s. Fifty-four Lincoln Mk.30s were built at the Australian Government Aircraft Factory in Melbourne. Some were used alongside RAF machines in operations against terrorists in Malaya.

Only one Lincoln, the B.Mk.15 FM300, was completed by Victory Aircraft in Canada after an order for 200 was cancelled following the defeat of Japan. FM300 first flew on 25 October 1945 but was subsequently placed in storage by the firm which had by then been taken over by Hawker Siddeley and renamed A.V. Roe Canada Ltd.

The Lincoln G-37-1 was used to test the 4,500 shp Rolls-Royce Tyne turboprop engine, the prototype of which was fitted in the nose. It flew past at the 1956 Farnborough Show on the power of the Tyne alone. Nine other Lincolns were used as engine testbeds, two for icing trials and another for radar and fire control development work.

The three civil Avro 695 Lincolnians for Paraguay had an additional ventral cargo hold. The machines, which were conversions of ex-RAF Lincolns, were scrapped when the scheme to transport meat fell through. Another machine was used by Argentina for south polar research while a further Lincoln conversion was used in the Berlin Air Lift.

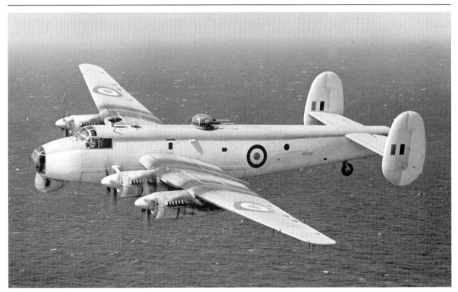

An Avro 696 Shackleton MR.1 long-range maritime patrol aircraft of RAF Coastal Command. The prototype Shackleton was first flown at Woodford by the Avro Chief Test Pilot J.H. Orrell on 9 March 1949. The type was powered by 2,450 hp Rolls-Royce Griffons and entered service in February 1951, replacing Lancaster MR.3s.

The Shackleton MR.2 had no gun turrets, a lengthened nose housing twin 20 mm cannons and a semi-retractable ventral radome. The MR.2 entered RAF service in Britain and Malta towards the end of 1952 and some remained in service until the early 1970s. Seventy-seven Shackleton MR.1/MR.1As and sixty-nine MR.2s were built.

One of eight Shackleton MR.3s delivered to the South African Air Force in 1957. The updated tricycle undercarriage MR.3 had an endurance of eighteen hours and thirty-four were built for the RAF. These entered service in 1957 and flew ocean patrols from bases in south-west England, Northern Ireland, Gibraltar and Malta, until replaced by Nimrods from 1970.

The final use of the Shackleton was as an airborne early warning aircraft. Twelve Shackleton MR.2s were converted to AEW.2 standard with the necessary radar being housed in a large ventral radome. The mark equipped No. 8 Squadron from January 1972 until the last six were finally replaced by Boeing Sentries on 1 July 1991.

The 6,500 lb st Rolls-Royce Avon RA.3 powered prototype of the Avro 698 Vulcan was first flown by Avro's Chief Test Pilot R. Falk on 30 August 1952 and displayed at Farnborough a few days later. Following trials, the initially straight wing leading edge was redesigned and the new shape adopted for all Vulcans from late 1955.

Delivery of the forty-five production Vulcan B.Mk.1s, powered by 11,000 lb st Bristol Olympus 101s, to the RAF began in May 1956 but it was not until July 1957 that the first squadron, No. 43 based at Waddington, became operational. Together with the Handley Page Victor and the Vickers Valiant the type formed the 'V' bomber force.

The Avro Vulcan B.Mk.2, eighty-nine of which were built, had increased span and more powerful versions of the Bristol Olympus engine. The first aircraft flew in August 1958 and the type entered squadron service in October 1960.

The Vulcan B. Mk.2 was designed to carry the Avro Blue Steel stand-off nuclear bomb, which could be launched 100 miles from its target. The first missile became operational in 1962 and from 1963 until 1967, when Polaris Submarines took over, three Vulcan and two Victor squadrons equipped with Blue Steel provided Britain's nuclear deterrent.

The Vulcan B.Mk.1 XA903 served as a testbed for the Olympus 593 engine used in the Concorde supersonic airliner. The aircraft was delivered to Bristol, where two other Vulcans had earlier been employed as testbeds, in January 1964. From 1973 until it was retired in 1979, XA903 was used to flight test the Tornado's RB.199 engine.

A Vulcan K.2 tanker refuelling a Panavia Tornado. To meet the additional needs for flight refuelling resulting from the Falklands War of 1982, six Vulcan B.2s were converted to K.2 standard and remained in service until early 1984. The Falklands War also saw the only operational use of the Vulcan. On 1 May 1982 a Vulcan flying from Ascension Island dropped a full load of twenty-one 1,000 lb bombs on the airfield at Port Stanley. Further ultra long range missions against the Argentinian forces followed.

An Avro 701 Athena T.Mk.2 three-seat advanced trainer. The fifteen production 1,280 hp Rolls-Royce Merlin powered Athena T.Mk.2s replaced Harvards at the RAF Flying College, Manby, where they were used for armament training from 1949.

VM129, the second of the three Athena T.Mk.1 prototypes, was powered by a 1,400 shp Rolls-Royce Dart turboprop engine. The other two machines, the first of which had its maiden flight on 12 June 1948, were powered by 1,010 shp Armstrong Siddeley Mamba turboprops. Non-availability of turboprop engines and changing requirements led to a change of specified engine and the development of the Athena T.Mk.2.

Six Avro 706 Ashton Rolls-Royce Nene powered research aircraft were built for the Ministry of Supply. The first aircraft, the Ashton MK.1 WB480, made its maiden flight on 1 September 1950 and was demonstrated at Farnborough a few days later. It was later used for high altitude research while the Ashton Mk.2 served as an engine testbed.

WB670, the last of three Ashton Mk.3s, flying with a Rolls-Royce Avon R.A.14 in a ventral pod behind water spray equipment for intake icing trials in 1955. The first Ashton Mk.3 was employed on radar bomb sight research while the second, which was initially used by the RAE at Farnborough, served as testbed for Bristol Olympus engines from 1955. The sole Ashton Mk.4 was also an RAE trials aircraft.

The prototype Avro 707 VX784 at the 1949 Farnborough Show, a few days after its first flight. The Rolls-Royce Derwent powered delta wing research aircraft was designed to provide data needed for development of the Avro Vulcan. VX784 was short lived, being lost in a crash on 30 September 1949. A second aircraft, the type 707B VX790, with a modified wing flew a year later and was used for low speed stability trials.

The third Avro 707, a type 707A, made its maiden flight from Boscombe Down on 14 June 1951. The machine, which had wing root air intakes, provided high speed data and after further research use was shipped to Australia where it flew until 1967. A second 707A was employed on general research at Farnborough from 1953 until 1967.

Like the second Avro 707A, the two-seat Avro 707B, was built at Avro's repair facility at Bracebridge Heath in Lincolnshire. Four such machines were ordered in late 1951 for delta training but in the event only one, WZ744, was completed. It was transferred to RAE Bedford in 1958 for supersonic tests and flew with a fly-by-wire control system.

The Avro 720 rocket-powered supersonic interceptor programme was cancelled in 1956 and the prototype scrapped when almost complete. Interception of enemy aircraft would have been on the power of an Armstrong Siddeley Screamer rocket engine fuelled by oxygen and kerosene, but it was also fitted with an A-S Viper turbojet for the return to base. It would have been equipped with De Havilland Firestreak missiles.

Sir Roy Dobson CBE was appointed Managing Director of the Hawker Siddeley Group, the parent of A.V. Roe and Co. Ltd, in 1958. R.H. Dobson joined Avro's design office in 1914 and became works manager only five years later. He progressed to General Manager in 1934 and became Managing Director of A.V. Roe and Co. Ltd in 1941.

G-ARAY was the second prototype of the Avro 748 forty-four seat short range airliner. Initially flown as a Series 1 on 10 April 1961 with 1,740 shp Rolls-Royce Dart 514s it was re-engined later in 1961 with 2,105 shp Dart 531s to become the Avro 748 Series 2 prototype. The maiden flight of the first Avro 748 G-APZV was on 24 June 1960.

Aerolineas Argentinas, the first airline to operate the Avro 748, took delivery of the first of its nine series 1 aircraft in January 1962. In Britain both Skyways Coach-Air and BKS Air Transport ordered the type before the prototype had been completed. The 748, the last aircraft to carry the Avro name, continued in production until 1988 and some 370 were built. Renamed the HS.748 in 1963, it was known as the BAe 748 from 1977.

From 1961 Hindustan Aeronautics Ltd at Kanpur, India, assembled 748s for use by the Indian Air Force and Indian Airlines. The maiden flight of the first HAL 748 took place on 1 November 1961. Four Series 1 aircraft were followed by eighty-five series 2 machines, the last of which was completed early in 1984.

Following trials with G-ARAY at Martlesham in February 1962, an order was placed for thirty-one rear-loading military freighter versions of the Avro 748 for the RAF. Known as the 748MF and powered by 2,970 shp Dart Mk.201Cs, the type equipped three squadrons. Ten RAF 748MFs were sold to the Royal New Zealand Air Force in 1976.

AVRO CANADA

An Avro Canada CF-100 Canuck using an experimental rocket pack to assist take off. In late 1945 Victory Aircraft Ltd, of Malton, Ontario, which had manufactured several Avro types during the Second World War, was taken over by Hawker Siddeley and renamed A.V. Roe Canada Ltd. The CF-100 single-seat fighter was the new company's first project.

The two Avro Canada CF-100 prototypes were powered by two Rolls-Royce Avon RA.2 turbojets rather than varying marks of the more powerful Avro Orenda that were fitted to production Mk.2, 3, 4 and 5 aircraft. The type, including some trainer variants, equipped thirteen RCAF squadrons while fifty-three were delivered to the Belgian Air Force.

The Avro Canada C-102 Jetliner was a fifty-passenger medium range transport intended to meet the needs of Trans Canada Airlines. The non-availability of Rolls-Royce Avon turbojets resulted in the aircraft being fitted with Rolls-Royce Derwent 8s and TCA withdrawing from the project. The maiden flight of the sole C-102 took place on 8 August 1949.

The prototype Avro Canada CF-105 Arrow supersonic fighter flew for the first time on 25 March 1958. Thirty-seven production aircraft with Avro Orenda Iroquois engines rather than the Pratt & Whitney J75s that powered the five development aircraft were ordered in June 1958, but eight months later the whole programme was cancelled.

Two Avro Model 1 Avrocars were built for the US Department of Defense and given the designation VZ-9V. The first machine was tested at Malton on 12 December 1959 but rose only a few feet. The second 'Saucer', which went to California for wind tunnel tests, performed no better and both machines were eventually donated to museums.

AVRO
INTERNATIONAL
AEROSPACE

The Avro 146-RJ series of regional airliners are updated versions of the successful British
Aerospace BAe 146. The revival of the Avro name took place in 1993 when British
Aerospace set up Avro International Aerospace at Woodford. Three models were in
production in 1995, the 70- to 94-seat RJ70, the 85- to 112-seat RJ85 and the 100- to
130-seat RJ100. All are powered by versions of the Textron Lycoming LF507.

Acknowledgements

I would like to thank my late father A.J. Jackson, whose outstanding collection of aviation photographs made this book possible. Sincere thanks are also due to the following individuals and organisations who have kindly provided additional photographs and/or information:

Avro International Aerospace • British Aerospace
J.M. Bruce (The J.M. Bruce/G.S. Leslie Collection) • The late P.T. Capon
Peter Connon • The Imperial War Museum • Philip Jarrett
Francis K. Mason • K.M. Molson • The RAF Museum
Rolls-Royce • Bruce Robertson.

Particular thanks are also due to my older brother, Wing Commander D.H. Jackson, RAF, for his support and encouragement.

BRITAIN IN OLD PHOTOGRAPHS

To order any of these titles please telephone Littlehampton Book Services on 01903 721596